WARS WAGED WITHIN

A MYSTICAL COLLECTION OF PHILOSOPHICAL POETRY

PARVI AGARWAL

Copyright © Parvi Agarwal
All Rights Reserved.

This book has been self-published with all reasonable efforts taken to make the material error-free by the author. No part of this book shall be used, reproduced in any manner whatsoever without written permission from the author, except in the case of brief quotations embodied in critical articles and reviews.

The Author of this book is solely responsible and liable for its content including but not limited to the views, representations, descriptions, statements, information, opinions and references ["Content"]. The Content of this book shall not constitute or be construed or deemed to reflect the opinion or expression of the Publisher or Editor. Neither the Publisher nor Editor endorse or approve the Content of this book or guarantee the reliability, accuracy or completeness of the Content published herein and do not make any representations or warranties of any kind, express or implied, including but not limited to the implied warranties of merchantability, fitness for a particular purpose. The Publisher and Editor shall not be liable whatsoever for any errors, omissions, whether such errors or omissions result from negligence, accident, or any other cause or claims for loss or damages of any kind, including without limitation, indirect or consequential loss or damage arising out of use, inability to use, or about the reliability, accuracy or sufficiency of the information contained in this book.

Made with ♥ on the Notion Press Platform
www.notionpress.com

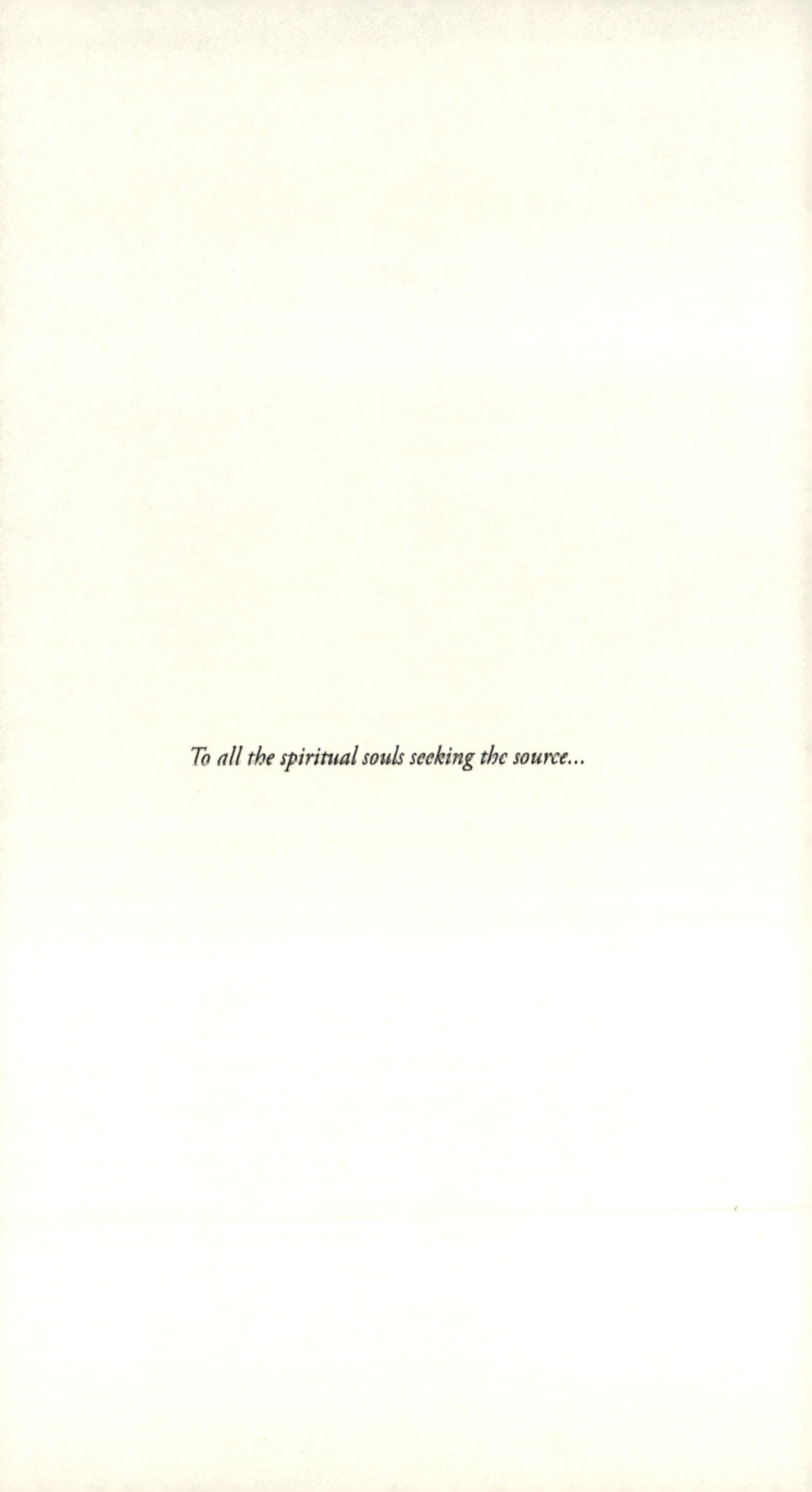

To all the spiritual souls seeking the source...

Contents

Contents

Contents

Preface

Dear seekers of wisdom,

Unfurling the essence of the divine has been a conquest of my heart since eternity... to reach the source, I got myself into philosophy, spirituality, human psyche, mythology and what not!

Admist theories and realities, explainations and experiences, I found my emotions to be the guiding light to the source. And this mystical collection of melodies is a song sung on the battlefield within... these are insights and intuitions seeping out from my mind to paper.

I wrote these verses between the age of 15 and 16. But claiming my work to be an effort of a few years would be unfair... As a believer of spiritual realities, I know that these verses are a culmination of limitless experiences and knowings, deep levels of consciousness and meditations and certainly a harmonious rhythm that pours from within.

This book is an attempt to give light to all those brave souls fighting inside, searching for reality beyond illusions... may this document find its readers and serve its purpose...

Acknowledgements

This book is not only my work but also a contribution of countless souls that have made me who I am... It is difficult to acknowledge just a few of them as my heart holds immense gratitude to every person who has been a part of my life's journey and has made me learn beautiful lessons.

With utmost reverance and elation I thank Shiv and all his creations...

But yes, I would indeed love to mention a person who played the most diligent role in the formation of these verses and that is my lovely sister Vasavi Agarwal. From my very birth to the recentmost breath, she has always been an inspiration, a gurdian angel and a forever supporting person... a hearty reader of all my poems, I am filled with the purest form of gratitude for her!

The following poem is a reflection of the dual aspects of our own selves. In the race to be masculine, we become too numb to emotions and pain. Hence we try to kill our negative aspects and traits rather than fixing them. We hate some parts of our own self that culminates to lack of self love.

Here I have expressed that we weren't expected to dislike any part of us fundamentally. We are allowed to be delicate, emotive and expressive. Killing or hiding any part of us was not required in the first place!

The sinister side represents our negatives. Shoulder portrays responsibilities. My right side, a representation of good and perfection is paradoxically hurting my left side. This poses a question against the purity of the right side, as it is represented causing hurt and pain.

The poem culminates with an introspective thought, that were we actually meant to hate ourselves so much? Is hating our negatives actually an act of positivity?

1. A Dagger in my shoulder

That wasn't difficult to force that knife

Right into my own shoulder... I sensed no strife

The pointed metal slowly slitting my feeble veins

There are multitudes of emotions around these pains

I keep digging the dagger on the sinister side

My bone screeches, this pain won't subside

I cannot walk further, I have lost my will

This wound on my collar, no ointment can fill

I built these wounds... never healed them

I killed my skin cause it used to feel them

And feelings I hate

Criticality... I appreciate

Been stabbing my shoulder to numb this feeling

I sway with no control... towards grieving

Then the wound takes the better part of me

Faints me... with some epiphany....

I get back my sight and the dagger is gone

I search for light... but it is not dawn

Was my sinister a demon or did I become one?

But a demon is sinister... perhaps my logics are undone...

I could not understand... this voice in my empty land
I took off those gloves that hid my harsh hand...
Since then I look at my shoulder every single night
From which side was I meant to fight...?
{Or was I really meant to? }
I think and think then I sleep
My hands are too harsh to wipe the tears i weep...

This poem represents that we as people, are afraid of ourselves, afraid of our inner truth. Why? Simply because we aren't open enough to unlimited possibilities. We are judgmental and narrow minded that adds up to our misery and pain.

Poetry is a way via which I portray my emotions. But I coat them with deceptive words and metaphors. This is a way that helps me to evade my reality and look at the truth in a softer manner. This is the reason I humorously criticize poetry. At the same time I accept the very fact that I am not bold enough to confront myself. I respect my poetic creativity because it is a part of me. Here I have represented self love and affection as well.

This poem is set up in humorous tone to showcase that self confrontation is an integral step towards self acceptance.

2. A Poem to Poetry

I got to know that I constructed some walls

Walls for myself to be inside

Walls for a soul that wants to hide

I learnt long back, how to bow

Standing up straight becomes an effort now

The words of exclamation lost my diction

Clinging to the bars in this prison became an addiction

My feet are hurt by walking on the gravel

But I don't spare my gavel, I don't spare my gavel

Could you expect this?

Can you accept this?

My inner voice questions and I answer in clear 'No's'

My eyes aren't strong enough to see the truth it shows

Euphemisms – oh the integral part of my element

The manipulative way for my conscious to supplement

This conflict – these wars inside –

I got to know my walls 'from' which I now hide!

Poetry! oh you caused me too much of pain!

I write you still cause you know I am insane

Cannot speak the truth so I use you as a tool

Well I never knew you were my explosive's fuel

Oh my great mind you make things more complex

Did you give my eyes a concave instead of convex
Well my cheeks get my metaphors well
That's how smiles and sorrows - together dwell
I laugh at you poetry, and I cry at my emotion
The medicine to this mayhem is a simple potion
The potion of truth that I see but don't accept
I neglect you my intuition, but you never neglect!
I am good at you poetry! But you do no good to me
You are a simple way for me to leave and flee
Still I respect you cause you are a part of me
(This statement can set all my things free)
But statements and feelings this time juxtapose
That is why I respect you and so do I oppose
Sometimes I think I should rather write a prose
But I learnt to bow, and my soul bows...

While walking on the path of self discovery, one day I realized, how I changed to be my dream self… but after evolution, people around me stopped recognizing me… I starting loosing the things I had to get everything I dreamt.

In pure unison of pain and success, I reflect, to think that is it a trap that I have fallen into? Or is it really the mountain I wanted to conquer? Unable to figure out, I surrender to my journey… with optimism… that nothing goes vain.

3. A Hole or a Mountain?

When they did not save me a seat
I felt it was my defeat
In arms of getting, I lose it all
I have many clothes, but I don't have a shawl
To protect me in the harsh winter around
I rise up but cannot touch the ground
I crafted this beautiful world for me
Some years down the lane I knew I was right
But I find myself strangled blissfully
In a game where there is no opponent to fight
This melancholic story is indeed subjected to laughter
I ran, I ran, and I always knew what after
I fought, I fought and I always knew what for
Seems like my situation is the most stunning metaphor
I made some conclusions but turns out they weren't right
I made some decisions that made me rediscover my sight
Cause the direction is same, the actions as well
I run, I fight still, but now I dwell
In a place where only I reside
I assumed it would be a fun ride
And sometimes, the assumptions are mighty wrong
Those times will be exactly when I'll again sing this song

Is this a hole I'm falling in?
Or is this a huge mountain?
Whatever it is, I know it's not vain
Whatever it is, I know it's not just pain
These are my assumptions once again
And until I find out what is true
I will search for white in the dark blue.

Self criticism over every single aspect of my life has been a major conflict of my heart since eternity... This piece of poetry portrays the complexity of my heart and the dilemma of seeing beyond the truth, but not the truth... The simple solution to all of this is self acceptance that still lingers as a conquest to my soul.

4. Written to Me

How can you find faults in a doc. I never submitted?

How can you accuse me of the crime I never committed?

Well crime is a realm I do and do not understand

But still in every situation, I do take a stand

I love-love reading between these lines

But reading these lines becomes hard sometimes

Duality, individuality – oh these mighty concepts

They leave me in pain, in agony in regret

To leave me to a level at which I beget

The essence of my being – which I still don't accept...

Blessed with two lovely sisters, my love at times becomes the reason of my guilt and sorrow... Expecting me to be their help always... wanting myself to comfort them always turns out to be a bane... When my baby sister stood up for the first time, she fell down, sobbing on the hurt... I accused myself of being irresponsible as I saw her weep in front of me...

In a greater context, this verse showcases how a soul has to learn its lessons alone... we cannot do anything when it comes to Karma, all we can do it be a support, a shoulder to cry on... becoming the victim of other's problems cannot be our part...

5. She Stands

Walked into my courtyard and I saw her there
She was never this tall, not even on a chair
She was trying to stroll
Just that and it was all
I was quiet and still, breathing in and out
But then I saw her fall
A short cry and shout
Weak knees and teary eyes
I could've saved her
Dark night with no light
I could have paved her
Held her hand tight to make her walk free
Could've given a shadow, to her under my tree
Where was I God? Just where was I?
Why did you have to make my love cry?
I know you want to teach her
To fall and get up again
I know you want to preach her
To bear a little pain
But she weeps in my arms
She cries until she calms
And I just wait and wait

Until she tries back again to gait.

The fire of agony, hate, anger and sizzling emotions inside of me, refuses to come out. Why? Simply because I am empathetic, someone who cannot cause others pain because of my negative emotions. My conscience stands against me, disables me to showcase my desperate state of mind. I seal the outlets of my emotions and allow the fire to burn every inch of the negativity... the inner conflict is indeed an excruciating pain, but I bear it, not only for others, but also for myself, to grow and evolve, to redeem my soul from the hate it carries.

6. Volcano

That deadly burning lava pent up inside
This rock-sturdy volcano tries to hide
It's boiling, it's burning, it's rushing through my veins
Explosion... explosion is in process again
[Suppress it, prevent it, just don't present it
Mix it, blend it, So that you don't repent it]
'Let that steam rise!'
That dynamic being cries
"Let it burn, let it corrode, let it dry up that inner skin
Incinerate every corner every speck of your sin
Let this swirl, let this raise you high
There is a lot of fire that won't let you sigh
It is not your choice
So do not try
They can't hear your voice
So do not cry
Burn! Burn! Do not roar
I invite you to my sacred door
Lie on the floor, let me take you out
Burn! Burn! Do not shout!"

Everyone has an inner child. That little emancipated voice inside. Being close to that inner child makes you realize the scars on its body. And healing those scars, soothing that little one it the first step to self evolution… This verse is not only about the childhood traumas that stain a soul but also about a young kid that does not know how to deal with emotions and wants to suppress them by forgetting…

7. I Swing her to Sleep

I swing on the bamboo that won't ever rust
I swing on the bamboo smeared with dust
I swing with a little life in my arms
She cries and cries until she calms
My bare feet on the warm floor
Like the rippling waves of the seashore
They are too afraid to leave the ground
I swing and swing with chaos around
Her little palm touch my skin
Her emotions speak through her wrinkled chin :-
"Placate me will you my elder one
I shouted, I wailed, but now I am done
Hum me to sleep, let me find my peace
I never knew that happiness was just another disease"
The weight of her eyelashes was heavier than her fears
Her eyes were moist, but they weren't filled with tears
I swing and swing until she forgets
I swing her to sleep before she regrets
I sooth her back with my palms
I will swing and swing until she calms

I wrote this when my pet fish died. I saw my younger brother deeply thinking at the death of the creature. Crafting the look on his face to words, and his questions into poetry, I wrote this one...

Truth is always appreciated, but sometimes, truth is hidden... not to delude us, but simply because we are too naïve, too small to know the greater plan...

Just like I couldn't tell the truth of death to my little brother, God hides the truth from us... only because sometimes, lies are spoken for the highest most loving good...

8. Truth?

He watches the aquarium as he daily does
Golden- white creatures making a bit of fuss
He counts them one to eight
He plays with them having faith
Faith that tomorrow as well
He will be able to count them all
But today he stopped at seven
And made a frightened withdrawal
Didi! Why is the 8th one floating today?
Is she sleeping? Is she tired? That is all he could say
How am I supposed to tell the 4 year old?
That she is lying in the arms of death
I think I think and then
I say it while I hold my breath.
She will be fine don't you worry dear
She will be alright don't you fear
I lied between the 12 year gap
I know...he knows... that it is a trap
How did this happen! His eyes are moist
He has doubts beneath his flinching voice
Do I....Do I have a choice?
To tell him that world isn't all about rejoice?

Tau ji! Did she eat well yesterday?
Papa! Are you sure she will be okay?
I don't lie but truth is harsh
I have ideas but my words are scarce...
Now he is lying on floor looking up at the sky
He is unable to comprehend whether it is a matter to cry
I have turned my emotions dry
But it is difficult for him to say goodbye
He will get up this evening once again
To count his lovely pets
I cannot look at him count till seven
I know he will cry until he wets
Wets his cheek, cause he is not meek
Not grown up enough to understand
That God has broken the strand
Strand of her life today
But I find it impossible to say
Say the truth as I always do
Cause he is 4... won't be able to get through..

Attachment is that feeling wherein you love something or someone so much so that you cannot even think of losing it/them. But attachment takes its most fierce form not when it is about things or people but when it is about ideas. When we are too attached to our own thought processes and ideas, and we know that they will be the reason of our downfall, we end up in a pendulum of emotional thinking... Being unattached, makes us flexible to evolve and grow...

This is a dynamic piece of poetry, that can be read with the perspective of attachment towards a person or an object as well, but it is meant to be read as a vere reflecvting attachments with thoughts.

9. Bamboo Plant

Why did I like this table bamboo
when I knew I will have to leave
Why did I made myself love it
when I cannot even share a sleeve
Why do I look at these green leaves
Everyday, when I know they will wilt
Why do I even love it
When I know it is a source of my guilt
I water it in regular fashion
With my heart I pour care
Why do I get attached
When I know it wont be 'there'...
There... where I am heading... and I want it to be with me
But I know plants covered in glass- we do not carry
Why did I get attached... why did I associate
When this world taught me this was inappropriate
Why did I nurture and sensed the nourishment
Why did I inflict to myself this punishment
I don't think plants feel... but I know I would
Oh god why did you not make me of wood
Now few days are left... and I cannot make a decision
Should I let it stay... or remove it from my discretion

I cannot decide... it is again a fight
God you gave me a lot... a lot of plight
I just wanted one plant...one to stay...
Why... why was is not okay
Why did my mind try to treat it like a herb
Now this wound...how do I curb?

Some take self expression as self victimization... no wonders I have been that one! In this verse I tried to spread the idea of the importance of self expression...it is done to know oneself; it is done to confront oneself... The power of self expression is the greatest one a human can have.

I love writing for the true sake of it... it brings me closer to myself, draws me in, sinks me to a meditative state from which I carve myself to be the person I want to be...

10. Write

Sometimes I ask myself... why do I even write?
Just to express this unsaid plight?
No...Dear no...Not at all...
I write to get up after every fall
I write to see what I cannot
I write to know my own thought [s]
I write cause I am very complex
I write so that I do not vex
People got no answers to the questions I put
I write to dream high and still ground my foot
With myself every day I sign a treaty
To get a step closer... closer to my deity
I keep filling these pages with my godly pen
I write cause writing is my Zen
I love to sink in these curves of ink
Cause paper gives me answers as I slowly blink
I thank this pen and paper every single day
These are the only things that never leave me astray
I write... I write... every single day
I write to understand the game that I play...

Temperance [self restraint] has been something that made me achieve almost everything I wanted… but then one day, I realised that temperance is for the slept souls… for souls who are unaware. Self restraint is an ornament for the dull souls but for the awakened ones, those who have sensed the true essence of reality, those who are aligned, those who refrain from things not because of restraint but because of awareness, temperance is just another chain onto them.

At the brink of self realization, when I found how temperance was yet another restriction clutching my soul, I found myself on a crossroad, unable to give up on something that has always done good but also unable to keep a habit that strangles my freedom. This poem is meant to make you reflect on what freedom actually is?

This poem asks you to ironically have temperance with the concept of temperance.

11. Temperance

Temperance is a memory
With which I am too attached
An etched melancholic history,
With some parts roughly scratched
It was a yellow garland on my dull dermis
The smell of which was an ethereal bliss
The seasons transcended the textures of my peel
Now temperance is rough with an uncomfortable feel
Is it an enchanting decor or just a simple noose?
Requires my valour, but it is just a choice to choose
Temperance is no concept that I can cram
At last I shrug, was freedom a mere sham?

Strong people, intelligent people, lovely souls are always looked up at... they are considered perfect by the society... No one knows the pain in their heart, no one knows the suffering they bear... and no one will ever know the story of their life.

Such gorgeous souls remain mistreated; no one comes to fill emotions in their cup because people assume that they already have enough love. Why would a strong man need care?

Expressing the feelings of a heart that is tired of being seen as perfect... tired of being backstabbed.... tired of having desires... tired of fake promises, this verse delves into the state of a soul that begs for freedom via harm, unable to cope by any alternate method..

This verse urges the people to understand that perfection is a hypothetical concept and strong people deserve emotional respect and empathy.

12. Can you please...?

Oh, is she still alive?

That poisoning...did she again survive?

This time you need to be a bit crude

Anyways this world is too rude

Nah... someone so strong does not need any care

This world isn't fair... at least you listen to her prayer

All that she is left to want now...

Pray! Let her have it somehow...

Tape her lips, rip that pink tint

Don't let her make noise or even drop a hint

Tie her hands with a tight thorny wire

Push her to the ground... build a pyre

Jab her heart as you stroke her hair

Slit her mind as you relieve her despair

Don't take that knife out, let it stay

Let blood and steel do the further play

Peel off her skin

Let her know she had no kin

Look at that mass of blood die in silent pain

Don't let even a drop in, as she wails for the rain

For the final end

Burn her in the furious fires

Steam your face with smoke
Smell the end of desires
Sense her departure... she will never return
Go away... don't let her yearn
Out of all the dreams she saw this is the only one
That you human can commence... please get this done
Burn her soul to ashes, drown her heart in tears
This is all she wants, please let her have it dear

Words are those subtle combinations of syllables that have the power to heal or wound... this composition emphasizes how compassion isn't always an element included in our words and how its absence it a struggle to my expression at times.

Befriending compassion is not an easy play but certainly not an impossible one either. Through this verse, I showcase my desire to always pour in compassion into my language every time I express.

13. Compassion isn't Courteous

Compassion isn't courteous to the art of articulation
He comes and goes- a subtle manipulation
I tell him to stay with my words forever
But dear Compassion, is kind and clever
He leaves my words like a soul leaves skin
These lines and curves mean no thing
Compassion isn't courteous to the art of articulation
Words can't tell my desperation, exasperation
My words seep to eyes, they see what they wish
But the Compassion that I type remains languish
I try to befriend Compassion forever,
But dear Compassion is kind and clever...
Compassion be courteous to the art of articulation
Dear friend stay with my words... in every situation
Make me a source of infinite creation
Let my world feel that utmost elation

*Crafting something with efforts and emotions requires a lot of valour.
Yellow, the colour that symbolizes actions, is used to represent the same
in the formation of a knitted cap.*

*However, the craft that I make does not turns out to be perfect, leaving
me worried that I will have to disentangle it again to make it better.*

*Emotional investments once done cannot be made again by scratch.
This leads me to berate my own immature creations...*

*In a deeper sense, the yarn is used as a metaphor for thoughts. This
piece of poetry showcases the distress involved in disentangling our once
made thoughts and redeeming our thinking process from preconceived
notions. Expressing the feelings of disappointment and vulnerability, it
deepens to the concept of emotional drainage involved in the same.*

14. Yellow Yarn

Yellow yarn and crochet hook
No that wasn't all it took
To craft this piece into a beautiful cap
But shades of yellow... feel like a trap
Pondering over the fibres of the yarn
Maybe they were built in a barn
This fabric is an itch to my sensitive skin
Sewing left some painful needles somewhere in...
Do I have to pull the thread?
And disentangle every strand?
Am I a poet who was never read?
And was still expected to stand?
It took me my life to make this art
Thought there won't be an end when it was the start
Pockets are empty to buy even twine
There is no colour I will ever call mine
But yellow yes... it is not a single shade
A beautiful caress... and at the end, a blade

In the pursuit of truth, when we actually find it, we question it continuously, neglecting our intuition and inner voice…that is exactly when truth stealthily leaves, leaving us again to learn some other lesson before finding it.

With the personification of Honesty as a bride, this verse showcases the beauty and attractiveness of honesty, that comes only when one is in a calm state of mind and leaves when the mind is engrossed in tumultuous emotions.

15. Deceptive Honesty

She comes in a veil, a beautiful bride
Smell of sunflowers and a scent sighed
Elegant walk, enchanting speech
I walk up to her to beseech
Who are you maiden? Can we talk?
Next scene is beach along which we walk
Her words so utopian, enthralling is her smile
She makes me gullible, swiftly agile
Who are you maiden? Why hide?
Mellifluously she says 'I am someone just and fide
They want me but they do not accept
They love me but having - they regret
They hunt, they scream, they die to be here
But everything in them culminates to despair
They call me beautiful just in my veil
I do not come in the season ruled by gale
I am passionately fiery and I am calmly cool
They want me but they prefer to be a fool
I do not hide, it is just they don't see
I am right here but they are not free
I am lethal as per them, a poison precise
I am the foetal element, this humanity defies

They call me deceptive but that is not my name
I am just a tricky- tricky game'
But... who are you maiden? I ask one again...
Her face is blank... a paper so plane
She walks away in that stunning gown
Does not bother to turn around
Oh! Where is my watch? I scream at her back
I lost my time tool... was my trust so slack?
She left me deceived, I don't know her name
Yes she was a tricky- tricky game!!

Big dreams, exceptional ideologies aren't manifested by just envisioning… they require soul-deep dedication that might make you lose your freedom, your true essence and even yourself.

This verse was written when I was on a mission to fight for my dreams… too afraid to become emotionless and mechanical in this entire process, I expressed my fears and willingness to work irrespective of my doubts and dilemmas, for the sake of my soul!

16. Before I turn into Machine

Before I turn into machine
I start seeing myself as mean
I become a tranquil serene
I just stop to intervene
Before I lose my heart
Lose the point of my start
Lose my aim- the dart
Encounter myself falling apart
I just wanna say that
In a marathon you don't creep
In summer you don't weep
In a station you don't leap
You aren't a Shepherd if you lose your sheep
Before I turn into machine
I start seeing myself as mean
I just wanna convene
That I will always be keen
To grow to sow
Whatever fruits I ripe
I will bow I will bow

I am not afraid to strive
Cause
In a marathon you don't creep
In summer you don't weep
In a station you don't leap
You aren't a Shepherd if you lose your sheep
Before I forget what is the nature
I forget I am amateur
I just forget my creed
I become the one who impede
Before I turn into machine
In a lockup I just lean
I just want to convene
I am ready to face the terrible storm
Chilly nights with moon in its frozen form
Even when I am exhausted
Even when I feel I lost it
I will sow, I will grow
Whatever fruits I ripe
I will bow I will bow
I am not afraid to strive!!

What is your perception of death? Is it negative? Is it purely destruction? Or could it be the most stunning experience of human life...? This passionate poem is intended to showcase the other side of death... Death is an emotion of pure peace... it can be felt even when you are alive...

In my spiritual path, I reached a divine point where life and death became one... where soul leaves the body but breath doesn't.... Death isn't only mystical but also very spiritual... dive in dear reader to change your perception of demise.

17. Desire to Die

I desire to die...

I desire to defy

The conventional definitions of death and time

I wish to die with the implication of this beauty pristine

Love from mind seeps to my chest

End of simple struggle, eternal rest

Nowhere to go... nothing to do

The shades of sky turn from black to blue

This is peace in which I desire to melt

Resting in peace... death I felt

I desire to die... at this perfect time

I desire to defy... the flavour of lime

I feel my soul ringing the subtle wind chime

She leaves my body... death feels divine...

Success is purely a perception... A big victory that felt nothing to me made me craft this composition as I went inside wondering why my heart was filled with the pain of failure when success was my reality.

Some unique perceptions may leave you all alone and misunderstood in the world... This verse is the voice of a soul that felt alone, a soul that felt misunderstood...and a soul that realised the power of perception!

18. Messed Up

Messed up soul, messed up heart
I land right back... did I even start?
I love spirals, but circles are not my taste
My emotions.... I am unkind that I waste
Drain, drain it is a dribbling rain
Pain, pain my heart aches with strain
So many words... left unexpressed
So many thoughts... left unaddressed
But the moment is gone,
They think I won
Was this all for which I was born?
Ripped is my soul, heart- it is torn...
Cannot be the refugee in my own heart
Do not call me a prisoner of the past
World swirls... quite-quite fast
Dear miser brain – looks aghast
Messed up soul, messed up heart
Eyes too moist-to see if I hit the dart...
Heavy eyelashes, strained brows
Mind weeps- unfulfilled vows
Mouth is sealed- can't process a word
Shattered trust- perturbed... perturbed

A heart afraid of being alone begs for loneliness one day... why?
Because that heart is too afraid to hurt...

This verse portrays how I became love... unable to prevent myself from
showing care and concern to everyone around but at the same time
unable to bear the pain of them loving me back...

Loving is courageous... loving is difficult... loving is painful... and
watching people go through all of this because I cannot help to separate
love from my element, I weep this poem...

Afraid to feel love, threatened by the idea of bereaving myself of the
ability of crying if I feel loved, I weep this poem...

19. Love not Loved

Can I please be alone forever?
And have no soul in my endeavour
I don't want people to be around
Silence is better than illusionary sound
I want to scratch my wrists... complaining I am alone
Because it is a pain... to have people who aren't home
It is better to be a victim...than a plaintiff with no proof...
I write this with a lot of thinking...that I want myself to be aloof
I am not cold... I want to be warm as tea
One whose warmth vanishes, rapidly
Just someone who comforts and passes by
Just someone who is permitted cry
Who is allowed to feel alone...
Even after having people near
Who is allowed to love
But never feels endear
I want to be hated... and still be kind
Don't open my eyes to love... I want to be blind
I want my ashes to blaze
With no skin to feel their heat
I want my soul to erase
Every inch of this beautiful pleat

WARS WAGED WITHIN

I want to smile the day death arrives
And watch people laughing while saying goodbyes
I want to be alone with no one near
I want to love but never feel endear...

This poem is a story… of beautiful death claiming a soul that thought of it as an escape… and Death seen as escapism is the most threatening myth!

Life is a karmic game, a cyclic story, a harmonious poetry…

20. The poem of Death

She embarked towards a cold balcony

To end an exhausted, excruciating journey

To take with her, the beauty of life

To take with her, a child of five

She perched on the edge, stroked the orphan's hair

She rattled with peace, and rocked on the gloomy chair

She swirled around the green trees

The calmness was felt in the dark breeze

Death was sweet, she smelled of wine

Her image was bleak with a unique shine

She sounded of rain

That would relieve his pain

She felt like the tranquility

That was beautifully insane

The young one was awake, ready to leave

"This world is fake", shouted his wet sleeve

Sitting straight, facing a terrible mirror

He took the pills with not even a single shiver

He shut the windows that saw that nasty world

He suffered terribly as his interior curled

She walked in the room, Moon shone bright

She embraced the gloom, every aspect of the plight

She offered her hand, with slightest of the strain,
Held his soul close, with the slightest of the pain,
Little did he know that this step was vain
Little did he know that life is cyclic game…

A world that glorifies strength suppresses tears... forgetting the magic of these drops that rinse our emotional burden.

This poem advocates normalizing crying... yes! Even if you are a man! Not every situation is under our control, not ever question has a reachable answer and not every misshap can be prevented.

But what will you do when you face vulnerability? Hide it? Suppress it? Or surrender it to nature...?

21. When she Cries

Ripples from her eyes, making their way to the cheeks

Amidst of all those lies, truth is all she seeks

Been running, wandering, crying in the dark

Those ripples were the music ... poetry of a lark

Moist eyelashes... dear red eyes...

She cries all alone... loneliness she hides

No complains... no questions... just pouring tears from her heart

They flow through time... dimensions that never start

This bitter water damning her skin

Her neck is too tired to raise her chin

The edge of the blanket is the only thing that appeases

Soaking all the pain that her pure mind releases

The soft wind brushes her eyes close

This is an eternal sleep... laden with a subtle prose

The last drop touches her warm ear

She surrenders to her dreams... they will hear

Her song of melancholy... and weave a dream divine

Her heart will release all that pain so sublime

Written as a farce to physics, a subject that I worked very hard on, this poem goes beyond the surface level interpretations.

Physics has been a subjected that I hated from my core... a subject I couldn't resist, but being a passionate learner, I gave my all to the subject, to conquer it, to love it.

Similarly there are situations, people, circumstances that we simply cannot appreciate, but for the sake of ascension, we fall in love with our enemies... not to defeat them, but to know them... to know ourselves better...

22. Mr Physics

I fell for the devil, the one that took my all
I fell for the ghost who taught me how to fall
He was a nightmare; I tried to morph to a dream
He was a death stare, but I left the threat unseen
Cause loving the devil is something unique
The depth in the darkness is what I seek
He strangled my throat and chained my wrist
But I raised a pen, never an angry fist
Cause he was someone, unloved and alone
I was testing my limits, to know someone unknown
I was trying to love someone who always exuded hate
I was trying to love someone whom no one would appreciate
People say he was a subject but he is an emotion I tell
Yes, he was someone, for whom I fell

*The rise of meditative energies is beyond explanations or expressions...
it is a divine experience, which is witnessed by a thoughtless mind, a
pure conscience and a balanced heart. It is a state of absolute trust in
the unknown, surrender to the spiritual forces and unison with the
soul...*

*This poem is an attempt to scribe the thoughts of a mind after
experiencing a soul...*

23. Something in my Spine

Something flows in my spine
Cannot taste but it smells of wine
Motion of ecstasy...feeling the divine
Something flows in my spine
Drop by drop I feel the upward motion
Thought by thought I let go of commotion
It flows like gentle waters... it flows through my mind
Felling of intoxication... I swiftly align
Something flows in my spine
Cannot explain but is feels divine
I don't know if this is drug or a drink
I am ready to fall from the topmost brink
And then I will sink...Sink in the twilight
And then I will let go of my sight
Motion and rest at the same time
Something flows in my spine

This melody is sung by a melancholic heart that is fighting everyday to find long lost peace... there are challenges in the way that aren't getting resolved after every means and methods...

Then at a point of reflection, I realise that I have always been fighting with myself, it's me who is the antihero of my own story...

Excess of awareness can be a disruption to existence because awareness comes at a cost of peace and paradoxically awareness leads to peace itself!

24. The Devil

I fight with a devil

one with no form or face

She isn't powerful

but holds a strong grace

I treated her with love, maybe she transforms

But devils ah! They aren't human forms

Then I presented my pleading request

But demons now! They are on their own quest

my tired soul begged for pardon

But seems like she waters poison in her garden

Frustrated I tried to wage a battle

But her powers are greater than my rattle

Yesterday... I asked what she wants

With no reply she still haunts...

I asked broken... who is she...?

She says she is no one but me...

That consciousness that I can handle no more

Who knew that she is a curse not a cure...

Who is Shiv, a deity outside or a consciousness within? Complete surrender and acceptance within, puts an end to the wars going on inside...

Wars cause death and destruction but only of the negativities, to leave behind a foetus to grow back again into light...

This verse is not only the final surrender to my deity but also an offering to him who has always been in my life in the most mystical ways and forms...

Om Namah Shivaya!

25. Surrender to Shiv

Mind is the only thing I have
And today...to you I give
This mind this body and this soul
I surrender myself to you my shiv
My Troubles... you patiently resolved
My Struggles...you valiantly strolled
You made me a medium that experiences what you give
And only to witness your poetry... here I live
This mind this body and this soul
I surrender myself to you my shiv
If you lay death upon me
I would drink it with passion
Dying how... I love it !
The most peaceful form of compassion
Take me away... sway me to sleep
I give myself to you as I slowly seep
Into trance...where you live
This soul surrenders herself to you shiv!

About The Author

Parvi Agarwal, whose name means beginning... was born in 2008 in a loving joint family of businessmen. Younger of the two daughters of Mr Raghav Krishna Agarwal and Mrs Anjani Agarwal, her childhood has been divine and insightful. An expressive soul, she started writing in search of truth and Shiv, at the tender age of 12. With high regards to wisdom, she believes that transformation can be accomplished via mere strokes of ink... A law aspirant, a philosophical thinker, and an emotive heart, she is an amalgamation of diversity. Her poetry is a mystical experience that is esoteric in its own way. *Contact: parviagarwal03@gmail.com*

www.ingramcontent.com/pod-product-compliance
Lightning Source LLC
Chambersburg PA
CBHW031646170726
47990CB00019B/2569